SECRET GARDEN AND OTHER POEMS

D1298691

Nitin Kakarla

Illustrated by Sarah Ross

DEDICATION

An ode to your love of books. This is for you Nivzii.

CONTENTS

ACKNOWLEDGEMENTS

Thank you for your reviews and kind encouragement –

Sindhakka

Sivamsa Pingali

Shoab Momin

Kayla Vasich

Emily Anders

The Notorious OsB

1. SECRET GARDEN

Young Colin had always been a sickly boy…

Crippled and bedridden, he felt like a broken toy…

And although the doctors could find nothing wrong…

He knew his limp feet would never get strong…

Out the window, at the Garden, he'd longingly stare…

Can't smell the roses, climb a tree, or get some fresh air…

"Is life even worth living, if it's so terribly unfair?"

At the corner of his teary eye, he caught something glary…

A tiny winged creature who was quite contrary…

Shone bright like hope, yet hopelessly scary…

"Are you a Pixie, Sprite, or a magical Fairy?"

"I'm all that and more, but do please call me Mary…"

"Though I dwell in your Garden, I mostly lay low…

Help the leaves sprout, flowers bloom, and the trees grow…

Could no longer bear your despairing gaze…

And ignore a burgeoning bud, whose soul decays…

I promise you'll walk soon, be no longer bedridden…

But before that transpires, we journey to a place hidden…

It's a Secret Garden, a realm of dreams you see…

Where the toil you put in, is reflected in reality…

All you must do there is pull out the weeds…

And in their place, you shall plant some rose seeds…"

As he had nothing to lose, Colin did as he was told…

They spirited away to the Garden, which was dark, damp, and cold…

The poor lad crawled his way to the weeds, replacing them one by one…

And the Fae cheered him on constantly until the day's work was done…

Every time he planted a Rose, felt better than the last…

Filled with more hope and resolve as each shift passed…

Light and warmth now flooded the place, the Garden began to heal…

Saw the strength return to his legs, in both the Imaginarium and for real…

Finally, the Secret Garden in his mind restored, Colin ran to his real one outside...

Without the Hope instilled by Mary, he wouldn't have even tried...

For where you sow Hope, which is akin to the Rose...

A feeling of doubt or despair, like the Thistle, never grows...

So, when things look bad for someone else, their outlook is downbeat...

Be that magical Friend they need, help them stand on their own two feet...

(Based on Frances Burnett's 'The Secret Garden')

Secret Garden

2. THE PURPLE ROSE

Trekking up a cold, steep mountain, was when I saw him the first time…

A lone, breathless, limping old man, making this perilous climb…

"O' Venerable struggler, might I just enquire…

Why in this agonizing state, you yearn to go higher?"

As he dragged himself up, with a leg clearly broken…

He said that he had to bring back to his wife, a loving floral token…

"A purple rose, that only blooms, atop this peak…

Is what I came here for, tis' what I seek…

It was up there, as youths, my wife and I first met…

Amid these roses, we made memories, we ought never to forget…

It was up there, that I got down on one knee to propose…

A penniless romantic, instead of a ring, I offered her a rose…"

To bring these lovers some joy, I thought I'd do my part…

For although I found his affections cloying, I respected his heart…

Stood tall in the face of adversity, his spine didn't cower…

So, I went up there by myself, and got him his damned flower…

On the way down, I had to carry him on my back...

For his irresponsibly foolish venture, I gave him some deserved flak...

And after we made it to the base, he started to cry...

With grateful tears in his eyes, he bid me goodbye...

Years later, at the same place, I chanced to meet him again...

Gaunt and feeble, he limped uphill, now with a walking cane...

"Do you have a death wish?", I confronted him aghast...

To reach the summit on a single limb, you've learned nothing from the past...

And why does your wife enable you to tempt fate?

She exhibits all the signs of a vain ingrate...

The old man failed to recognize me at first...

But as soon as he did, succumbed to a woeful outburst...

"When I last saw you, my wife was sick in her head...

Couldn't speak or recognize me, from her mind her memories fled...

Thought if I presented her the rose, it might revive her...

Its purple shade, its dewy smell, might some memory stir...

She died soon after, with me a stranger in her eye…

Though she's long gone now, I can't let her memory die…

And now that I've started losing my own mind…

Once more a purple rose, I need to find…

So please help me up there, if you can be so kind…

And as my wife's memories have me to this earth bind…

If the purple roses can't recall them, I'll want to be amidst them, left behind…"

The Purple Rose

3. MR. ADONIS

Mr. Adonis goes to a Surgeon to get his eyes fixed...

"I have trouble judging distance, and get my colors mixed..."

The Surgeon then said to him with a gleeful distaste...

"The eyes aren't your biggest flaw, though they are awkwardly spaced...

Let's start with the head, and make our way down...

Your ears stick out too much, there's no hair on the crown...

The nose is too crooked, the lips too thin...

Pockmarks all over, and a clear double chin..."

"But I need to see better", the patient exclaimed...

"There's need for naught else", he said slightly ashamed...

"My face is not perfect, there's plenty that's wrong...

But I've come to be attached to it, as I've had it this long..."

"The neck needs a lift; the tummy deserves a tuck..."

The Surgeon further diagnosed, without giving a fuck...

"And although you seem accustomed to your blunt features...

The pretty ones are treated better by this World of shallow creatures..."

"Then perhaps it is the beholders that need their eyes sorted...

For I am perfect the way I am" Adonis retorted...

"Won't deface a valuable remembrance for the sake of another...

As I'm the last living semblance of my lovely late mother...

The only surgery you would perform if I did what's on my mind...

Is dislodging my forceful foot from your impertinent behind..."

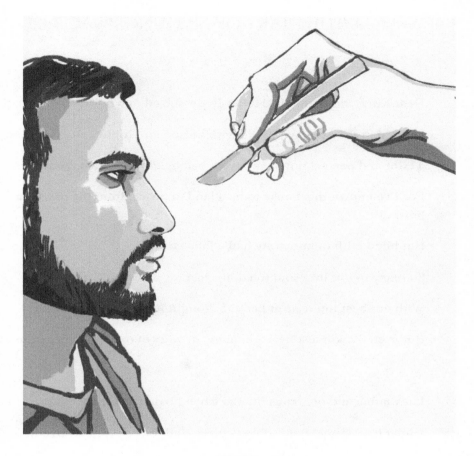

Mr. Adonis

4. THE DIARY OF A YOUNG ROACH

Dear Kitty, this is the final letter I've resolved to write...

Hidden in the attic, paralyzed with poison and fright...

Terror and persecution, I believed, belonged to an era bygone...

For I've known this house to be a land of peace, from the day I was born...

But blind faith in humanity had a fatal cost...

So many of our lives and freedoms lost...

With our best interests at heart, I thought he'd never surrender...

But even the kindest hearts change, in sway of the opposite gender...

How noble and generous he was when he first arrived...

Under his regime, our numbers grew, and the economy thrived...

Liberty – To roam the realm, not just at nights but even the day...

Equality – He even shared the bed in which he lay...

Fraternity – Proffered the half-eaten Pizzas and Parfait...

Women invaded rarely, but our nation always resisted...

They retreated shortly after, moved by how wonderfully we coexisted...

But this harmony finally shattered, when that ghastly woman appears...

A murderous plague personified, more fearful than our worst fears...

At first, with slithery sweetness, she presented exotic food to taste...

What was accepted as a gesture of goodwill, was with lethal poison-laced...

Turned the press against us, with her vile, baseless attacks...

As she rolled up the newspapers and conferred brutal whacks...

Finally retaliated with our air force, one landed in her hair...

She jumped and shrieked, we had her thoroughly scared...

Our troops then occupied, all the dresses she'd wear...

Gave her an apoplectic fit, this was war – and all was fair...

All this while our human, did naught but helplessly stare...

She moved cautiously for a while, wary of what trap she may step in...

But alas, just as we relaxed, attacked us with a chemical weapon...

The last one left standing, my experience most traumatic...

I escaped just in time, scarcely alive, into this attic...

As one human brutalized us, though we meant her no malice...

Another stood by and watched, I deem to be equally callous...

But I take solace in the human condition, your inevitable doom approaches...

When you've wiped each other out, who is to inherit Earth but us meek roaches...

The Diary of a Young Roach

5. THE CHIVALROUS SON

Takes three generations to make a gentleman they say, in this case, it took just one...

A philistine father who struck it rich, he had such a refined son...

And although he bought him everything he asked for, that money could buy...

The teenager still moped 'round the mansion, uttering an occasional sigh...

"What's brought on this melancholy?" the concerned dad inquired...

"My bank account at your service, buy anything that's desired..."

"Some things in life money can't buy, most priceless of which is love...

Your millions won't get me what I seek; what I need is providence from above..."

"Have faith in your old man and his cash, sonny...

To solve any of life's problems, I'd bet my money on money...

If you've placed her on a pedestal, it's time you brought her down...

Let her know you're her better, your father owns the town..."

"An objectionably outdated outlook!", said the son clearly pained...

The fancies of a modern lady, in his resentful tone explained –

"She isn't hung up on facets that are skin-deep…

The foremost requirement would be that he not be a creep…

Not entirely faultless, his faults be benign, however…

Who is just clever enough for her, but not especially clever…

More than a brooding genius, a happy idiot they'd choose…

Who treats her with regard, respecting her earnest views…

Likes her appropriately, but not too much…

Not a bit selfish, a man with a soft touch…

Who gleefully accepts what's been offered, asks for no more…

And most crucially of all, he ought not to be a bore…"

His urge to utter objections and ridicule, his father bravely fought…

'Experts on relationships, have likely never been in one' he thought…

Apologized for his ignorance, and probed about this girl he sought -

"She's the reason I traded the comfort of my car, for a bumpy bus ride…

A sophomore commuting to school each day, another always by her side…

I'd like to sing her praises, but end up talking about the weather…

How can I say anything more, we barely have time together…

When will I ever get to confer with her, when can I - my love confess?

Your money cannot buy me her time, can't rid me of this stress..."

The lovelorn lad came to his dad, a week later, beaming ear to ear...

"My love requited, due to a strange happenstance, it would appear...

Boarded the bus to discover, that the only other passenger was her...

Soon halted on the highway, as for an accident did occur...

Stuck in the traffic for hours together, we did nothing but talk...

And as the sun was setting, we got off the bus, hand in hand we walked...

It was charm and luck, not your boorish ostentation, that helped me in the end...

You can never buy class father, despite all the money you spend."

Fetched his checkbook, as soon as his son left, he had folks to pay...

A hundred each for all the passengers, that decided to not board today...

To the men that faked the accident, a thousand bucks apiece...

For maneuvering this entire farce, ten grand to the chief of police...

There was no reason to tell his chivalrous son, that his love was based on a lie...

For his happiness meant the world to him, another thing money can't buy...

The Chivalrous Son

6. ALEANA

The cultural capital of the world, the greatest city ever built...

The sights and sounds could soon get old, its charms may yet wilt...

But there's something here that will make me return, something I can't jilt...

The sight of her smile, the sound of her laugh, her gait with the drink unsplit...

Wandering aimlessly down the crowded 7th street...

Bored and hungry, stiff-backed with aching feet...

Walked into Pig n Whistle for a swig and some meat...

Irish luck rubbed off on me, things now looked upbeat...

A sweet personality, a kind soul, one may estimate through her eyes...

Too good for me I felt, I gave up with a sigh...

We'd pair up just as well as whipped cream on Shepard's pie...

Still love to see her from afar, without raising my hopes too high...

Shakespeare didn't limit his work to a private diary scrawl...

Van Gogh wasn't content with painting his bathroom wall...

The aesthetic treasures of this world were meant for one and all...

But how I wish I could reserve the pub from winter to fall...

Aleana

7. THE FROG PRINCE

As a young lady walked past a pond, a frog doth spoke...

"This is no dream fair maiden, you are indeed woke...

A handsome prince I once was, now as an ugly thing, I croak...

Kiss me and break this curse, turn me back into a bloke..."

"A strange plea indeed this is, and faith I do lack...

Even if I trust your words and give your lips a smack...

You have to first convince me, why should I bring you back?"

"For I am a beautiful prince, who is soon to be king...

There are songs of my charms that bards still sing...

And I'll make you my wife, oh pretty little thing...

Help bear you some princes, what joy they'll bring..."

"You assume too much sir; you cross the line...

You offer to espouse, and I must decline...

Any weird fancies, to yourself you must confine...

I alone choose who I love, no one's decision but mine..."

"Then I will give you riches, make it worth your while...

You'll never need to work again; you'd live your life in style...

Even if you spend it all, I'll restock your treasure pile..."

"I will make my own fortune, to no one I am bound...

Even if I fail in this, self-worth I shall have found...

Your offers don't convince me still, none of them profound..."

"It's your loss then, be that as it may...

I will go to the forest, there is a Dragon I must slay...

And an ugly Witch, with her magic tricks, also must pay...

Burn at the stake she will, for making me this way..."

"The forest is protected by the Dragon, who's lived there from the start...

He scares the humans away, who want to tear his home apart...

And the Witch brews Salves, Potions, medicines - she is plenty smart...

Never turns away the sick or poor, she has the kindest heart..."

"Now I understand why she cursed you so...

Made you ugly on the outside, so that humility you will know...

A woman worth her kind, would never a kiss bestow...

On a Frog or a pretty Prince who has an ugly soul..."

The Frog Prince

8. ONE FOR SORROW

One for sorrow, and two for bliss...

An old rhyme about Magpies, I reminisce...

So akin to people they are, who until too late, chase after shiny things...

Knowing full well that without love, we're but birds with broken wings...

Now that you're gone, I gaze at the heavens, where we'll reunite...

The Magpie, who shares my pain, also looks to the starry night...

Strewn among the trinkets is the shiniest pearl you'll ever see...

Perhaps the Moon, with its bright veneer, a Magpie heaven be...

The lonely bird wants to join her love as soon as she can...

To escape this unworthy world, she came up with a plan...

To fly into the horizon, however distant it may be...

And reach the Moon before it descends into the sea...

Flew all night without rest, not a wink of sleep in her eye...

But the Moon dissolved before her, as sunlight filled the sky...

Nights turned to days, Seas became lands uncharted...

But the Moon was no closer than it was on the day she departed...

As days turned to weeks, she felt she was back where she started...

And no longer, from her companion, she could stay parted...

Thus, as the Moon drowned into the Sea, where the whole day it spent...

So did the longing bird, who made the fatal descent...

To love her mate to the moon and back, the Magpie so tried...

Likewise, my love, I'll soon take the plunge, see you on the other side...

One for Sorrow

9. THE CHRISTMAS GIFT

'twas the season of Melancholy, the least wonderful time of their year...

The festive lights and the merry snow couldn't fill the poor couple with cheer...

Over the jingling bells and the catchy carols, only the cold, barren wind they hear...

It blows into their eyes with futile malice, those already filled with tears...

For though the partridges nestled together on the pear tree, they still felt alone...

As much as they tried, as much as they prayed, they couldn't bear fruit of their own...

Long been building a nest egg for this, and had worked themselves to the bone...

But they remained childless another year, the elusive Stork's whereabouts unknown...

'Perhaps we ought to celebrate a little' thought Mary on Christmas eve...

'To mourn yet another Christmas would be wasteful, just because I can't conceive...

Unlike erstwhile years, I should get Joe a nice gift this time...

But apart from the savings for my absent babe, I'm down to my very last dime...'

On her way back from work, she saw an ideal gift at the antique store…

It was the perfect chain for the pocket watch that her husband wore…

Her mind made up, she entered the Wigmakers shop next door…

As he was proud of this family heirloom, he wore the watch everywhere…

So, for his sake, she mournfully sold off her lovely, long, luscious hair…

Made just enough to buy the chain, with nothing else to spare…

She went home, and waited anxiously for Joe's imminent return…

'He would loathe my tiny hair, and schoolboy semblance' she thought with concern…

And when he did come home and glanced at her, he stood at the door aghast…

"Do you find me ugly without hair?" Mary then tearfully asked…

"I assure you, my love, that it is not your appearance that astounds me," Joe said…

"You are beautiful, even if hair lost on your head is gained as your beard instead…

It's just that I didn't want to dip into our savings, so I sold the pocket watch I flaunted...

And bought the jeweled hair combs – the ones that you've always wanted..."

Recounting their misfortunes, the couple sat down for dinner with a sigh...

Unbeknownst to them, a Christmas miracle conferred – they've earned the gifts of Magi...

And as they gratefully supped on their modest stew...

A new life within Mary demanded she eat for two...

(Based on O. Henry's 'The Gift of the Magi')

The Christmas Gift

10. PROCRASTINATION

Welcome to my country, the republic of procrasti-nation...

Where you've come to escape work, and have an endless vacation...

To the North lies Leisure Lake, to the South – Isle Do-it-tomorrow...

Its capital city is Napville, where you find no regret or sorrow...

Plenty of distractions adorn these streets...

Another show on Netflix, or the Orange King's tweets...

Some of these attractions you once found boring...

Are so much more interesting now, you can't stop exploring...

One thing that goes missing here is your reflection...

As there's no need to improve yourself here, no need for perfection...

And although your future self will hate you for this...

Don't think about it now, ignorance is bliss...

But if you feel you've overstayed your welcome, to your goal you must retreat...

If you want to be Successful - Learned, Rich, Famous, Artist or Athlete...

Follow my advice to escape this place, and beat this lazy trap...

Umm... er... I'll get back to you on this one after I've taken a very quick nap...

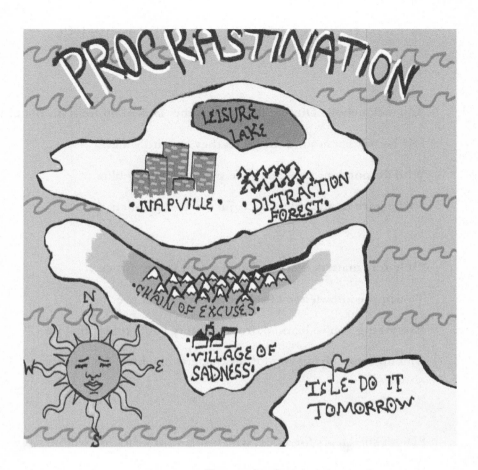

Procrastination

11. DINNER WITH A PHILOSOPHER

At a melancholic Dinner, the Philosopher looked up from his plate...

His Family sat around the table; they all hardly ate...

With despondent faces, they were clearly feeling blue...

So, he gave them futile advice, just as Philosophers do...

"It hardly matters that you failed a test, young Bruce...

To acquire knowledge of subjects you'll never use...

Everything you've learned, from memory you'll promptly lose...

End up a complying cog for the Societal machine, from this sad abuse..."

"Don't shed tears for a boy, who broke your heart you willfully gave...

With bittersweet Love, my girl, there's joy to be had and pain to be braved...

A square peg and a round hole, don't each other crave...

Choosing an ugly kind man is better than a handsome knave..."

Finally turned to his wife, still foggy as to why so sullenly she behaved...

"It's because living with you, is a thankless chore...

You give us logic and reason when empathy is called for...

Can't keep up this pretense, can't take this anymore...

I'm leaving you for another, I'll soon be out the door..."

"I'd like to show passion, but for me, it's too late...

So, I shall with the same stoic tone, this parting counsel state...

If you get a good spouse, you'll find happiness anew...

But if you don't, you'll become a philosopher too...

Now let's get back to the Dinner I made, let's all have a taste...

There's no point letting good Hemlock go to waste..."

Dinner with a Philosopher

12. CHICKINFERNO

'Abandon all hope, ye who enter here..."

Etched on its door, that I passed through with fear...

The house of pain, filled with guttural screams...

Was I indeed in hell? Or is it one of my dreams?

With no Virgil to guide me, went forth on my own...

To reap in death, the sins in life sown...

Within these circles of hell, what horrors awaited...

With what ironic punishments, had I been fated?

First came Lust - where you forcefully bred...

The offspring created, to an archfiend fed...

Next was Gluttony – to quench an insatiable thirst...

Made to constantly gorge, until you all but burst...

Shackled in cages, there were none too large...

For all my Pride, wallowed in own discharge...

It was fiery Wrath that soon followed Pride...

Thrown in scalding hot oil, was left to be fried...

Then came Violence, was torn limb from limb...

But the torture didn't end there, turned even more grim...

"Dinners served!" yelled the wife, and he woke up in cold sweat...

Realized it was but a nightmare, he was under no threat...

Mr. Rooster cautiously went to eat, still panic-stricken...

"What's wrong with you?" inquired Mrs. Hen, "You're actin' like a chicken!"

Soon forgot about the dream, as he dug into his plate of food...

"Mmmm... Why the hell do these humans have to taste so good?!"

Chickinferno

13. FELIX FELICIS

Felix had an uncommon trait of having common sense...

But he was drunk enough tonight, for it to be briefly dispensed...

As he staggered out the bar, he noticed the street dweller...

Who beckoned to join him, looked quite the harmless feller...

"Pick a card, and see what your future holds," said the Fortune teller...

He went along with the gag, did Felix, humored him by picking one...

But things soon turned grim, the context no longer fun...

The psychic turned it over, to reveal the eerie form of Death...

Examined the palm next, he turned pale and was out of breath...

"Unless you cause someone's demise, you shall part from the person you love...

You cannot avoid this macabre fate, as it's written in the stars above...

But perhaps it might help if you buy this decanter of liquid luck...

Although it looks and tastes like sugar water, it is well worth the 100 bucks..."

When you let a fib or half-truth latch on to your mind...

Wicked biases work on them, till certainty in them, you'll find...

Pondered the prophecy as he wandered the streets, had revoked the effects of Rum...

The maudlin fantasy of the night had at dawn, sobering reality become...

'I cannot part from my dearest Rose, thus I am forced to kill...

But I have no enemies, nor hate anyone, none who fit the bill...

Perhaps, it is time I visited my old Aunt Jill...

A lonely alcoholic, who often drank to her gills...

Gift her the Seer's green bottle, in which I have some poison-filled...'

The Aunt promised to try it later, as at present she was ill...

So moved by his kind gesture, that she later changed her will...

A few days later, the old woman had lost her life...

She had left all her possessions to her nephew and his soon-to-be wife...

With misfortune averted, Felix finally proposed...

Left all the planning to his bride, his innocent Rose...

Amusingly enough, the Aunt's house was the venue she chose...

It was a fine, cheery night when they tied the knot...

Made possible by his dead Aunt, Felix sadly thought...

So grateful for the gifts received from the house's former host...

Rose had even included her in the wedding toast...

"Your Aunt really drank the place dry", she then whispered after a sip...

Realization struck him late, as the groom raised his glass to his lip...

"This green decanter was the only one left untouched..."

Were her final words spoken, as her own neck she clutched...

Felix Felicis

14. LES MOTS COMPTENT

Walking on a lonely beach, the time – a few hours past heartbreak...

The stars in the night sky held up like candles in lost love's wake...

'How I wish to be like the sea!', I thought, as its breeze gently wiped the tears from my face...

As she constantly effaces the words writ on its shores, so could words from my mind be erased...

Words can inspire as well as destroy...

They have the power to bring boundless joy...

Kind words are worth much, and cost little...

Cruel words are costly, and not worth spittle...

They can lead you to deep despair...

especially when spoken by someone for whom you care...

And as my feet soaked wet, the air cleared my head...

Words harshly carved in my mind's shores recalled all that was said...

In quixotic pursuit of closure, we each had to say our benign piece...

But with emotions brought to the boil, it ended with malicious release...

Was told that I'm too full of myself, my ego needed deflation...

Qualities once admired, now deemed sly affectation...

At first, I was called a dull and uninspired bore...

Soon progressed to label me a heartless and unfeeling whore...

Our memories together corrupted, my heart already broken...

Braced for the parting gift, the harshest words spoken...

Every one of which was sharp as a knife, into my soul they twisted...

'The world wouldn't miss you, it would be better if you never existed.'

Grief is the ultimate price one pays for love...

The heavy heart drags you 'neath the surface, courage forsaken above...

And under misery's oppression, I further sink...

Gasping for a breath of hope, my lungs doth only despair drink...

I drown slowly into sleep now, submerged under sorrow...

Perhaps the pain will subside soon, there's always hope in tomorrow...

Woke up from this bleak dream, in a beautiful field of golden rye...

My love lay beside me, gazing up at the light blue sky...

Gentle, warm words filled the air with remorse, forgiveness, mirth...

My heart feels so light now, my body floats up off this Earth...

Swaying like a light, transparent cloud, towards the heavens I drift and swerved...

Such peace, such happiness I felt, this is more than I've ever deserved...

Les Mots Comptent

15. THE THREE WISHES

Once at the Crossroads, did I chance to meet...

A mangy vagrant, who begged for some food to eat...

Bought this pitiful tramp, some pie, and ale at the inn...

He then revealed his true self, transformed into a Djinn...

"As a reward for your generosity, I'll more than repay you in kind...

Grant you any three wishes, that come to your mind..."

Couldn't believe my luck, and I said with immense glee...

"I've only ever craved happiness, so as far as I can see...

Eternal Wealth, Health, and Love would be the obvious three..."

"Before I grant you this, I need you to think twice...

To avoid any regrets, you should follow my advice...

Use up a wish, and at your future, take a peek...

See if you've found the happiness you seek..."

Curiously convinced, I did what I was told...

If I stuck to my wishes, I saw what would unfold...

Immortality, a mountain of Gold, and the Woman of my dreams...

I had all I wanted, but all was not as it seems...

The endless wealth did my ambitions, quell…

With immortality, my zest for life fell…

And love without a free will wasn't love at all…

Retracted my wishes, after seeing what's to befall…

Perhaps to the days bygone, a visit need be paid…

Avoid causing or being hurt, change some decisions I made…

So, with my next wish, I wanted to change my past…

Would that unburden my heart of regret, bring me joy at last?

Lessons learned from past mistakes; you apply tomorrow…

Caution and Empathy bloom in the harsh desert of sorrow…

So, Although I changed my history, according to plan…

Couldn't help feel that I've become a different, lesser man…

"Should've asked you this from the get-go…

So, with my final wish, this is all I'd like to know…

Show me the path to happiness, be my spiritual guide…"

To which the omniscient Djinn thus replied -

"There's no happiness like the tranquil joy that Gratitude brings…

And though you are out of boons…

Luckily, it comes to you, the moment you stop wishing for things…"

The Three Wishes

16. THE MOLE

'A diamond with a flaw holds more allure than a pebble without one...'

Thought the Earth, beholding the shiny orb, that for her had faithfully spun...

'For these charming imperfections, make life exciting and fun...

His attention, love, and light are for me alone, barring none...'

In each other's company day or night, at first, they loved with vigor...

But with proximity, the love spot, this mole, seemed slightly bigger...

'These defects seem less endearing, they could be slightly bettered...

The personality that shone freely, need be rightly fettered...'

But the blemish became more evident with each passing day...

As stormy clouds loomed on the horizon – dark and grey...

'Perhaps we can only be friends in fair weather...

Thought I'd cure you of your faults once together...'

'Now your every form and shape, I find jarring...

All I can see now is your hideous scarring...

In essence, we're together, but our minds estranged...

Your pockmarked soul, why won't it change?'

'The Moon eclipsed in the end, there's naught but darkness...

Not until it's too late, I reach an introspective starkness...

Put one among the stars, on a pedestal, they're sure to fall...

Love only if you accept them as they are, flaws and all...'

The Mole

17. THE LUCKY VAGRANT

Down on his luck, forced to dwell on the cold Boston street…

A vagrant – new to his ilk, devoid of food, deprived of heat…

But not wholly bankrupt of pride, wouldn't feed off public teat….

Instead, the prison was a much finer prospect, he reasoned…

All he needed was to commit a minor crime, no high treason…

'it's the state's obligation to feed and shelter me this season…'

Fine dining and dashing, would have the cops deliciously baited…

Whilst being lavishly sated until he was happily inmated…

But the host at the restaurant had his scheme undone…

For his tattered garb, he was haughtily shunned…

A lewd proposal to lone women by the shops…

This bold maneuver must surely invite cops…

The first woman was all too keen to have some fun…

Another whacked me with a bible, turned out a nun…

Driven to the edge, he confronted a cop on his beat…

Plucked up courage, cursed, and spat at his feet…

'Another drunk fan! There's no harm done...

It's all in good fun, for the Patriots have won...'

Lastly, filched a street vendor's hat on the run, left him uncrowned...

Turned to note that he couldn't give chase, for he was wheelchair-bound...

Realization struck, the Vagrant stopped in his tracks, deeply ashamed...

The industrious vendor unlike him, though missing legs, had dignity unmaimed...

Perversely thankful for own state, witnessing the plight of another....

'With no criminal record, I can turn my life 'round, given my druthers...'

A sudden tap on his shoulder intruded rosy thoughts of salvation...

'You're arrested for Loitering', said the cop, 'We're off to the station...'

(Based on O. Henry's 'The Cop and the Anthem')

The Lucky Vagrant

18. THE OLD PAINTER

On a crowded Manhattan sidewalk, yet another face he sketches…

A master of his craft, he was happy with the few dollars it fetches…

Although a thriving portrait artist, he was in the days of his youth…

He resented his job, for he needed to obscure the truth…

As his vocation demanded, countless faces he drew…

These visages to the soul had subtle secrets, that his practiced hand knew…

The eyes could range from intelligent, determined, or of charming wit…

To the dull, mirthless, and lacking grit…

The smile could be confident, honest, or warm…

Or of a shy, deceptive, or cold nature inform…

Even the nose turned up or the resolute jaw had a story to tell…

And not all was said with the mouth but with the manner as well…

Couldn't depict with all honesty what he had discerned…

Thus, by portraying his subjects ideally, a living he had earned…

But presently his conscience objected, as his life's canvas now frayed…

No longer were his subjects, for their vanity, falsely portrayed…

Only rough truth delivered through the caricatures he made…

As a true artist despises all that is insincere...

He magnified the truth of every disingenuous face that appeared...

Depicted the bigoted holy man with lecherous eyes...

In a sea of men, being passionately baptized...

The Wall St. banker and the car salesman with their deceitful toil...

Drawn with a fitting analogy of selling snake oil...

Deceitful women with shallow men, lured them with their siren songs...

Deceitful men with caring women, liked to frivolously string them along...

This embarrassing imagery, in their subjects, had seeds of doubt sown...

To guard themselves against the lies of others or stop believing their own...

But there's one class of charlatan, the painter could never deride...

With practiced inauthenticity, his true face, he'd hide...

His heart could be dancing with joy, though he was teary-eyed...

His voice ever unwavering, as he expertly lied...

Though devoid of morality, they don't lack for projection...

Every question countered with deflection, the masters of misdirection...

The politician who comes begging for votes every election...

Held up a mirror to his face, his caricature was his own reflection...

The Old Painter

19. ISKANDAR

The young King and his army set out to conquer the World...

Death and destruction commonplace, where his banners unfurled...

Followed his father's footsteps, seeking more of what he sought...

If a greater kingdom must be forged, more battles need be fought...

More victories need be won; to this bloody path, he was bound...

Until he reached the edge of the land - until Oceanus be found...

Instead, he found the fountain of youth with his early death...

Immortalized as a great conqueror, he breathed his dying breath...

Ascending to the Heavens, alongside the Angel of death, was the King's soul...

As he looked upon the World he departed, he questioned, within it, his role...

"How will I be remembered? He asked his new divine friend with wings...

What is my contribution to humankind in the grand scheme of things?"

"As a human, you were a microcosm of humanity, the angel said...

These questions you pose, you should've asked yourself instead...

A human is not his physical self, evolving until he dies…

So, the monuments that cast your fame, will disintegrate likewise…

A human is not the memories he holds, he loses them with time…

So will your history be rewritten, heroic exploits turned to crimes…

But biases and instincts he retains, even if his memory he'd lose…

Certain impulses that arise, when given certain cues…

Your legacy to humanity is the examples you've set…

The inclinations passed onto the generations you beget…"

"Your penchant for war and greed, that you so held in merit…

Just as you did from your father, your posterity too will inherit…

Your kingdom built on corpses, your monuments on slave's backs…

On this fiendish path you've paved, they'll follow in your tracks…"

"Although ambition and victory, in your endeavors emerge…

To repeat said atrocities, these values will urge…

Grand intentions don't justify vicious deeds…

This is how your will to the World reads…

For the flowers of war, you've planted the seeds…"

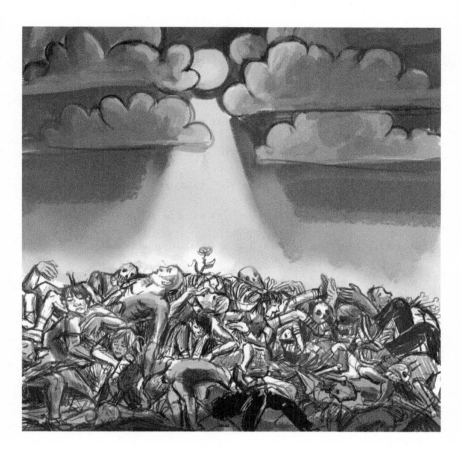

Iskandar

20. SOCIAL MEDIA

Had my first taste at college, more than a decade ago...

Since then, I've only seen this vile addiction grow...

At first, I used, on an odd dull day, just to stay connected...

Neither my work nor relationships were in any way affected...

Liked Charlie's one-liners, Molly's music, and conversations with Mary J...

Felt I could give it up cold turkey, get off the stuff any day...

Now I'm always on it, it's gotten to a point of abuse...

Created a brand-new persona, just to garner more views...

Pretend to be happy and have lots of fun, I do it all for the gram...

Stand up for causes I care nothing about, hashtag #My life's a sham...

Someone take my damn phone away; I need an intervention...

Need to get back to reality, and stop with this pretension...

If you've also hit rock bottom, it's time to call it quits...

Real drugs are safer in comparison if you need those Dopamine hits...

♪

Social Media

21. THE INCREDIBLE STEINER

The incredible Steiner was my only friend and hero when I was a kid...

Appeared out of nowhere in times of distress, otherwise, he'd stay hid...

He could become angry, fearful, or even turn sad...

No one else believed he was real, said I was mad...

Soon, his terrible outbursts had landed me in the hospital one day...

They gave me medicine to recover, and Steiner got locked away...

These pills made me numb, losing my only friend was easy to bear...

Didn't think much of my hero thereafter, I didn't seem to much care...

This new disposition attracted new friends, and with them came new habits...

New drugs, added to the ones prescribed, helped an older me chase white rabbits...

With this deliberate release of happy chemicals in my brain...

Life's stresses along with Steiner were yet to be seen again...

A more mystical dependence took hold, as time passes...

As a remedy for my substance abuse, I took the opiate of the masses...

My eyes opened to religious ecstasy, as they were blinded by faith...

And life's anguishes and Steiner left me alone unscathed...

Sought a different type of bliss soon after, the one of the marital sort...

But that was impermanent too, as bereavement cut it short...

The sudden loss of a child, our love couldn't have sustained...

Deemed heartless for being stoic, I showed no signs of being pained...

For without the darkness of sorrow, brilliant joy could not be discerned...

My unfeeling soul had finally, for my friend's homecoming yearned...

Gave up all of life's soothing addictions, their safe contentment spurned...

Cleansed my body and mind of poisoned panaceas, for my hero's imminent return...

Dormant feelings inside of me erupted in a volcanic release...

Sadness and rage unconfined, have broken through my façade of peace...

Screaming and crying, though strangely gratifying, Steiner had finally returned...

Hidden in plain sight all along, his identity I had finally learned...

For he had always been the real me; the placid alter ego an inhuman pretender...

Sorrow, anger, fear, and consequent relief, poured forth in earnest splendor...

Elastic emotions pulled back for too long, will break you, if you never surrender...

So, in my mind's cemetery, I had dug up deeply buried emotions without a misgiving...

Realized that an unexamined life, fraught with addictions, is not worth living...

So, I carved a new headstone there, and had not a single tear shed...

For it was my false self who slept here evermore, his epitaph is what I've read...

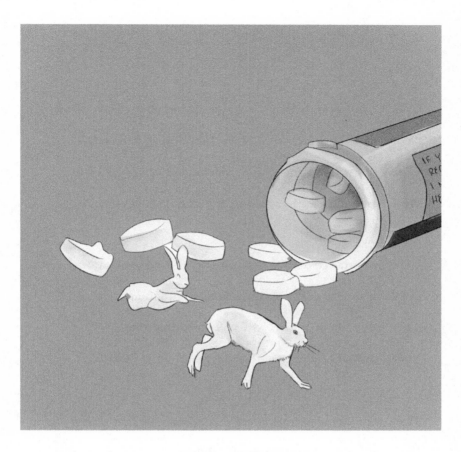

The Incredible Steiner

22. LOVE'S LABOUR'S LOST

Once Cupid said to Death when they had chanced to meet...

"Your avid overwork does my entire purpose defeat...

I can't scheme, for the young, to love and create new life...

While you kill them by making war and disease rife..."

"The importance of love, said Death, you do overstate...

Humans don't need your intrusions to procreate...

They value life over love, as I will soon illustrate...

Visit a mortal on their deathbed, to settle this debate..."

They approached a frightened girl, whose life had all but ended...

Death offered, on one condition, to have her time extended...

As long as you don't fall in love, seal it with a kiss...

You can go on living this life of passionless bliss...

But if you aren't careful, and let your guard drop...

Your eyes shuttered, you'll be out of breath, your loving heart stop..."

Inviting Cupid's arrows, meant Death's Scythe would follow suit...

So, youthful inclinations did she from her own heart uproot...

Her teenage years went by, she had never been on a date...

A host of men courted and coveted, she never did reciprocate...

But her steely heart yielded to one disarming smile...

Its bearer was kind and true, with such elegant style...

Lavished her with love, which she repaid in kind...

Willing to pay dearly, for breaching the fateful pact signed...

Past caring of consequences, closed her eyes, and did her lips part...

Prepared to never wake again, kissed her beloved sweetheart...

Held tight in lovers embrace, eternal darkness she anticipated...

She slowly opened her eyes, heart pounding, her breath unabated...

Cried tears of relief, as Death who never came...

Renounced her love bestowed life, he obliged to claim...

"When she closed her eyes, and their love was, with their lips sealed...

He took her breath away, her heart skipped a beat – as was the deal..."

Said Death to Cupid, as he concluded his *cruel pun*...

"Your remarks proved true, you have this contest won...

For those in love, will henceforth, evade my deathly pall...

As they'd rather love and lose their lives than never to have loved at all..."

Love's Labour's Lost

23. THE INSTALLMENT BABY

The miserly Scrooge got the most precious Christmas gift...

From his estranged daughter who had thrown off his yoke of thrift...

Against his wishes, she married young, and they drifted apart...

But with the birth of her child, they sought a brand-new start...

So, she invited the new Grandfather to her fine suburban house...

And prove to him, that she wasn't wedded to a good-for-nothing spouse...

It seemed to Scrooge at first glance, that all was well...

Jack and Jill had a healthy child, their life seemed swell...

He'd judged his daughter's life choices harshly, he ruefully mourned...

When he saw their big house, which was with lavish furniture adorned...

'But how could they manage to afford all of this?

All was not as it seemed, there was something amiss...'

He had never known Jack to hold on to a job...

Had he won the lottery? Which bank did he rob?

Firstly, into the living room, Scrooge was led...

"Make yourself at home", his son-in-law said...

When the news on the TV started to hurt his head...

Scrooge asked if he could switch to the sports instead...

"We bought this in installments", sang Jack on a merry note...

"The television is paid for, but not the remote..."

'How odd!', thought Scrooge, 'But nothing to fret about...'

'A one-off case of indulgence, no doubt...'

Perhaps it was best, to give his tired eyes some rest...

So, the esteemed guest, put his musical fingers to test...

But to play the piano with his grandchild sat on his knees...

Would've only been possible, if it wasn't missing the keys...

"We bought this in installments too", Jack chimed with glee...

This was not a rare hasty purchase, but a rash shopping spree...

This never-never nightmare didn't stop there...

Owned nothing in the house, except for the air...

Their modern fridge had everything but a door...

Some tiles were absent on their varnished floor...

The chairs' legs, like the clock's hands, went missing...

The toilet had no seat to sit on while pissing...

Their grandiose nest when laid bare...

Was but an inescapable creditor's snare...

Scrooge had seen enough, it was time he went...

His patience, in installments, was all but spent...

Jack would've offered to drop him off in his car...

But a steering wheel and two tires can't get you much far...

'Be frugal, be free', wise counsel imparted...

Wrote them a big check, before he departed...

Gratefully welcoming this generous gift bestowed...

The couple wished to pay off one of the many debts they owed...

"For the expenses of childbirth, said Jill, we took out a medical loan...

Let's pay that off first, and our child finally be our own..."

(Based on Ruskin Bond's 'The Never Never Nest')

The Installment Baby

24. THE GREAT HIKE

I walk this path of no return, knowing not where it will lead...

Yet with faith infused Spirit, I shall march on at Godspeed...

Through wind and rain, my dreams tossed and blown...

Yet with hope in my heart, I will never walk alone...

I may falter now and then, unable to move along...

Yet resolve shall renew the spring in my step & on my lips a hearty song...

Journeying alongside me are people of every shape and size...

All on their unique paths toward the same summit in the skies...

The privileged few glide on the smoothest trail, fitted with cozy boots...

While some others drag their calloused feet, over the more treacherous routes...

Lost count of the gnarled roots I tripped over, the jagged stones painfully felt...

Yet I will never complain – there's no use! Just play with the hand I'm dealt...

My body aches, my soul wearies, with the passage of time...

More responsibilities on my back now make for a burdensome climb...

Midway to the peak, I question the choices I've made...

Did I make a wrong turn in the past? Perhaps somewhere I've strayed?

Yet I am optimistic of the future, though my heart's laden with rue...

I catch my breath for a bit, and enjoy the glorious view...

I limp along, my bones in agony, my mind failing bit by bit...

There's no reason to go on, I could end the suffering here, and quit...

Just then I heard a voice from above, one with familiar grit...

'Have you no regard for your own blood, tears, and sweat?

Never give up! Just look how far you have come', said the descending silhouette...

Soak your feet in the river above, with a grand view of the Sunset...'

These words gave me new hope, banished my lingering fear...

I could hear the river atop now, nature's music in my ear...

Turned around to thank the kid, who did magically disappear...

Made it to the promised peak, after what felt like a lifetime...

Even with all the toil and hardship, it was well worth the climb...

A tall ash tree, with shining dew, that stood forever green...

The river of life flowing by it, was clear and pristine...

Mirrored the wondrous setting Sun, shimmered with a golden sheen...

Then recalled the kind words from the stranger, whose face I'd barely seen...

Just like the Sun's kindness, makes the bare moon glow...

One's compassion can uplift another, more than you could know...

And as I sat peacefully, by the serene riverbank...

I gazed upon my reflection, and realized who to thank...

I met the apparition of my younger self, having just recalled the face...

I had to take care of myself, give myself kind solace...

Being kind to yourself and others makes the World a better place...

The Great Hike

25. THE JASMINE TREE

She was growing up so fast, blooming in her Life's Spring…

It's time I had that dreaded talk, her Mother thought, with my sweet little thing…

"This secret I divulge now, my own mother once told me…

An incantation, when uttered, turns you into a Jasmine Tree…

Then someone you trust, and consented to use the spell…

Will apply it once more, transform you back to a Belle…"

She met a special friend soon enough, who would her heart steal…

Placed in him her earnest faith, she did her charm reveal…

Embraced him with youthful fragrance, let him bask in her loving shade…

He then recited the spell, and turned her back into a maid…

But soon her scent seemed overly sweet, he took her shade for granted…

She observed this dispassion, which left her quite disenchanted…

Although she wanted out, he just couldn't let her go…

"A farewell tryst one last time", he said clinging to her bough…

No harm in this final rendezvous, at least this to him I owe…

They met away from prying eyes, as was his plan...

If I can't have your fragrance, he thought, nor would any other man...

As soon as she transformed into the Jasmine tree like she always did...

He revealed his true nature, he so slyly hid...

Crudely picked all her flowers, left her branches broken...

Abandoned her in tree form, the spell left unspoken...

In her arboreal guise, she couldn't utter a sound...

But mother's intuition led her to be found...

The sobbing parent lifted her curse, made her human again...

With a broken, maimed exterior, within it a far greater pain...

The agony of betrayed trust, of a heart cleft in twain...

"Misbelieved that my fragrance is recalled fondly by the one it adorned...

But the stench of Malice drowns it out when the person is scorned...

If there's another life, I hope I'm as a cautious Rose reborn...

Be a gentle flower among flowers, and among thorns, be a thorn..."

The Jasmine Tree

26. THE CROW

In a wintery town, its avian denizens were condemned to be harshly fated...

But a quartet of birds among others scarcely survived, never migrated...

The Nightingale, born with musical talent, went hungry with no patrons to captivate...

Rose through the ranks with flattery and charm, the Parrot couldn't fill itself with idle prate...

The oft-doted Peacock, ever rewarded for its beauty, was also starving today...

But the common Crow, for whom struggle wasn't uncommon, had food stashed away...

Whose working-class struggles others had looked down upon with scorn...

With no beauty, charm, talent, or a silver spoon it was born...

And although the others thought it beneath their dignity, to ask the Crow to share...

Their corvid cousin was all too glad to offer what it could spare...

Though deemed a pitiful fare, none of the others had turned up their beak...

And as they devoured on the Crow's meager savings, he was happy to just be part of a clique...

Soon scant of food, scant of luck, in this abundance of snow…

To find better rations, the Parrot had demanded of the crow…

"With no more of your scavenged scraps, we ought to be restocked…

You need to do much better to be part of our noble group" he squawked…

"We could ask the Grocer if he could spare some meat…

But it is beneath my standing to brazenly entreat…

Unlike my song, said the Nightingale, which is lush and ever so sweet…

Your raucous caws should invoke a pitiful charity of something to eat…"

"An empty house with an unlit hearth, we ought to raid…

Through the chimney, you'll descend" to the Crow the Peacock bade…

With the infamy of the deed and the soot, my esteem and fine feathers would fade…

But yours already blackened with ignominy can hardly further degrade…"

Soon it was Spring, and the land had once again become abundant...

The Crow no longer needed, was once more a bad omen, made redundant...

To be part of a showy clique, he had stooped to beg and steal...

But what's earned through honest toil, will always make for a better meal...

And as his opportunistic friendship abruptly concludes...

He learned that there were no menial jobs, only menial attitudes...

The Crow

27. THE ENTERPRISING ANT

Took the road less trodden, did one enterprising ant…

While the blue collared others worked hard at the plant…

And as they drudged on with the leaves, taking no breaks…

The enterprising ant luckily found some cakes…

He promised the rest, that they would get their fill…

Only if they bowed and scraped to fulfill his will…

Got rich enough to buy his own anthill…

But the enterprising ant was unhappy still…

I'll have them all enslaved, he finally thought…

He burnt down the plant as was his wicked plot…

Now they must beg me for cake, as it's all they've got…

He finally found peace as he bought himself a yacht…

The kid with the ant-farm, who saw the situation as dire…

Flooded it with water, to put out the remnant fire…

The enterprising ant safely made out on his boat…

While the rest perished with no leaves on which to float…

They have their cake and eat it from their Ivory towers...

The Ultra Capitalists will destroy the planet of ours...

Leave us to die, as they go colonize the Moon or Mars...

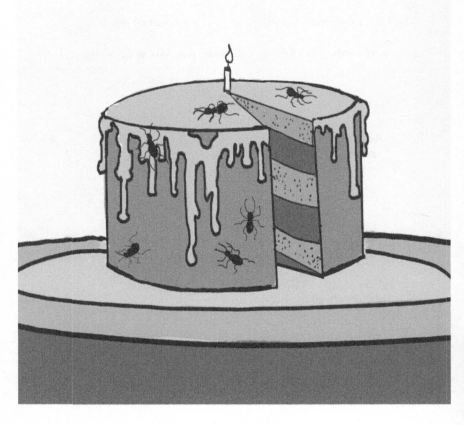

The Enterprising Ant

28. NATALIE'S LULLABY

Like the pitter-patter of your unborn feet, that fills me with glee…

So special will your ephemeral imprint on the World be…

Soon free of my tender prison, your hands unfettered…

They will mold this world into someplace much better…

As you lie in my nurturing garden, still yet to bloom…

A bedtime story I recite to you, the flower bud in my womb…

The tale is about me, your mother Earth, the joys, and sorrows I hold…

Prepare you the best I can for life, don't say that you weren't told…

The World a double-edged sword, good and bad that cut your heart asunder…

At first, as a child, only hunger and sickness you'd know…

But still, look upon this World with unfading curious wonder…

Then in adolescence, you are full of angst and woe…

Yet you feel invincible, with the hormonal spell you're under…

Crippling failures and searing heartbreaks you will never forget…

But even with the blinding pain, it's still worth opening your eyes to love…

In your prime, you are worked to the bone, but may still end up in debt...

Toil akin to Sisyphus' curse, but you will find self-worth on your way above...

Finally, with old age comes wisdom, along with frailty and sad regret...

But depending on where you are born, it could all get much worse...

And who you are born as, can also come as an inescapable curse...

Race, creed, and class may act as your life's bane...

Your sex, and who you love, may bring you vicious disdain...

Although there are many things in this world, you'd abhor...

Friendship, love, kindness, laughter are all worth living for...

And if you're still unhappy with the World, if that's the case...

Be the change you wish to see in this ever-changing place...

You add inherent value to the World, simply by existing...

An irreplaceable cog in its machinery that can't go missing...

Illuminating life however briefly flickered is vital for the warmth it gave...

And shone a light onto the path for humanity to further pave...

Your empty cradle would weigh heavier on me, than your eventually burdened grave...

Natalie's Lullaby

29. EGO

A hungry Monster from its cerebral confines freed...

Gave you the ability you desired, if only you let it feed...

As the World was large, it split into two, did the beast...

One went on a trip to the West, while the other to the far East...

The Monster that went West first possessed a member of the Mason's guild...

Gave him such talent, that a beautiful Cathedral, he did build...

He also got into the Smith who forged the sharpest swords,

And the Wordsmith who had great skill with words...

The Tailor who stitched some dazzling cloaks,

The Jester who told the funniest jokes...

Heads bloated, with untamed pride, of these good and honest folks...

The Monster outgrew all of them, its hunger unquelled...

And then went in search for another soul in which to dwell...

It finally decided to ensnare someone, where it could feed the longest...

So, it sought out the richest, most powerful, prettiest, and the strongest...

As it encircled the Globe in its search, met its twin on the other side...

Listed its conquests and plans, with an ironic sense of pride...

To which the unimpressed Monster from the East then replied-

"Find yourself someone who feeds you unconditionally, my dear twin...

One who thinks himself better merely due to the color of his skin...

Another who paints himself holier than others, absolved of any sin...

Or the ignorant, who argue against logic with their very smug grin...

For these be the heads that will be eternally empty within...

Where you have no danger of ever running out of space, or go starvin'

Ego

30. ART

Three patrons visited an Art gallery one day...

For the divine painter had his abstract work on display...

Divided the critics, with his very mysterious ways...

While some rejected him and had nothing good to say...

Others prostrated themselves before him to pray...

First of these patrons, was a young scholarly type...

Stared at the painting with disinterest, declared it meaningless tripe...

"The painter's design and colors both seem quite random...

His intentions unclear, none can understand him..."

The second was a lady with sad vacant eyes...

Claimed she knew exactly what the artist implies...

Tries to convince herself, as much as she can...

That each tiny brushstroke is part of his plan...

A young girl, merry and curious, came in at last...

Was struck by the beauty of the colorful contrasts...

The happy Yellow, the mournful Grey, the tumultuous Red, the peaceful White...

The dark despairing shadows, that enhanced the hopeful light...

"I don't care about the deeper meaning, only concerned about how I feel...

Because the work of an Artist and his Art is to help the soul heal...

I'm happy to experience this feeling, happy to be a part...

Of this beautiful life, that imitates such fine art..."

Art

31. DETROIT

A city personified by the old workhorse, lying on the hospital bed...

Saddled by capitalistic malaise, he looked out the window, saw the disease spread...

To this once-thriving city, as a strong-willed youth, he came hither...

Now, along with the autumn leaves, both the man and city wither...

Peered across the street, at an abandoned building, with its bright red wall...

In front of it, a lone tree, looking weak and helpless, as its starved leaves fall...

As the fever left his mind morbid, a strange fancy he conceives...

The city he loved was the dying tree, its deserting residents were leaves...

Each falling leaf drained a little more life from him and the city he cherished...

Appointed himself the last leaf, and when it fell, he too will have perished...

As winter came, the conditions at their worst, only a handful of leaves were left...

And then there was only one, still yet to drop, make him of his life bereft...

The despairing cold couldn't snuff its fiery resolve, and on the tree, it remained...

For each passing day, with its refusal to fall, new hope the man had gained...

Then sprouted two, three, and more, it was an optimistic surprise...

Smack in the middle of winter too, he couldn't believe his eyes...

Convinced that it was a sign, and inspired by the way the tree had fought...

He too refused to give up on life, he gave it all he got...

Sunny days were finally here, as he had weathered the woeful throes...

As soon as he had recovered, went to admire the tree up close...

Stunned by this strange revelation, he had nearly fainted -

What he thought he saw from his window, was but a mural painted...

And before it, the real thing stood naked of leaves, as it should be...

Its lush growth a mirage on the wall, of a beautifully rendered tree...

It was art that had healed and inspired him...

His last refuge of hope, when things turned grim...

This city turned canvas, shall also recover...

Its leaves will return, its fortunes reflower...

Art is the highest expression of the human spirit, resilient to any ordeal...

Gives us hope until spring arrives when the trees will once more bloom for real...

Detroit

32. THE QUACK DOCTOR

A cure for my affliction, I searched far and wide...

Chanced to come across his name, in the classified...

He claimed to be a Physician of the soul...

Could heal all wounds, and make you whole...

So, in a desperate need to get back to my prime...

Paid a skeptical visit to this Dr. Time...

He inquired about my symptoms, and I began to explain...

That many torrents of torment, pooled into a sea of pain...

"Growing up in a broken home, which in itself was no good...

Added to the bullying at school, made for a traumatic childhood...

My bleak teenage years were defined by repeated heartbreak...

Along with the betrayal of friends who turned out to be fake...

The sufferings of my youth, now thoroughly upstaged...

By the terrible experiences of my now middle age...

Mourned the unbearable, untimely loss of my pet...

Alimony for a failed marriage, I'm swimming in debt...

Work bears no meaning, life's lost its thrill...

So, no matter the expense, I'll foot the bill...

Try anything to ease this pain, injections, or pills..."

Wearing a stupid smirk, the Doctor blankly stared back...

Started to suspect that the fellow might be a quack...

Produced a club out of nowhere, gave my head a right whack...

After I woke up sometime later, gave me an explanation and an icepack...

"My patented treatment, administered with my cane...

Promotes the loss of past memories, and substitutes the former pain...

And although you may never again be right as rain...

Newer wounds will replace the old, time and time again..."

The Quack Doctor

33. GUILTY CONSCIENCE

An invisible crown suddenly appeared on my head...

It wouldn't come off, forced to wear it to bed...

Gently prickled like the summer heat at first...

Applied a soothing fib, to have it nursed -

My actions, in retrospect, were surely justified...

Did nothing wrong, I reasoned, with false pride...

Soon it got heavier, burdened my head underneath...

Let me just make amends, and lose this cursed wreath...

I can feel good about myself at last...

When I receive the forgiveness, I've asked...

What's done is done, I can't change the past...

Hope it doesn't undo the goodwill I've amassed...

Now it whispers in my ear, doesn't let me sleep...

whatsoever a man soweth, that shall he also reap...

I deserve this punishment, in torment I weep...

Still unrelieved from the crown, further into my head it seeps...

It has finally addled my wits, has driven me mad…

But of one thing I am relieved, of this I am glad…

To never repeat my past mistakes, did the best I could…

I'm a different man now, I've changed for the good…

Although, it matters little, whether a reformed life was lead…

This crown of thorns, cast in guilt, is to be worn until you're dead…

Guilty Conscience

AUTHOR'S NOTE

Hi, I'm Nitin.

I've never actually read a poetry book myself (or gone past the first few pages at least), simply because the most popular poets use highbrow language and their works have deep, subtle meanings which I could never totally comprehend.

What I've tried to write here are mostly simple stories with hints of irony and humor.

I hope you enjoyed reading this book!

Made in the USA
Monee, IL
17 October 2021

80185346R00069